A Cat for William

Pamela Garcia

Please remember to leave a review of my book at your favorite retailer.

Star Dust Dreams
Copyright © 2017 P. R. Garcia
All rights reserved.

www.prgarcia1.com

DEDICATION

This book is dedicated to William, who allowed me to tell his story.
A source of inspiration, he fights every day against a disabling disease.
And to Pippin, a gray tiger cat, who came into his life and makes William's life more bearable.

This is

WILLIAM

William lives in the small town of Merkville

In a valley surrounded by snowy mountains,

On a quiet little street,

In a cute white house with a a red front door.

William is a Jazz Musician.

He travels the country
Singing the Blues,
Playing music on his guitar
And sorrowful notes on his horn.

But what he loves the most

Is playing the piano.

William is happy.

He has the best life.

But one day William became ill.

And the doctors told him he could not play in his Jazz Band anymore.

William was very sad.

After several months, he came home from the hospital

To a very different life.

When he felt well enough
William spent time outside
Enjoying the sun on his face,
Listening to the birds sing
And smelling the flowers.

When he was too sick
He stayed in bed.

Often in pain, he watched as the world
Seemed to pass him by.

He wondered what the future would bring.

Would he ever get better?

Would he ever have a normal life again?

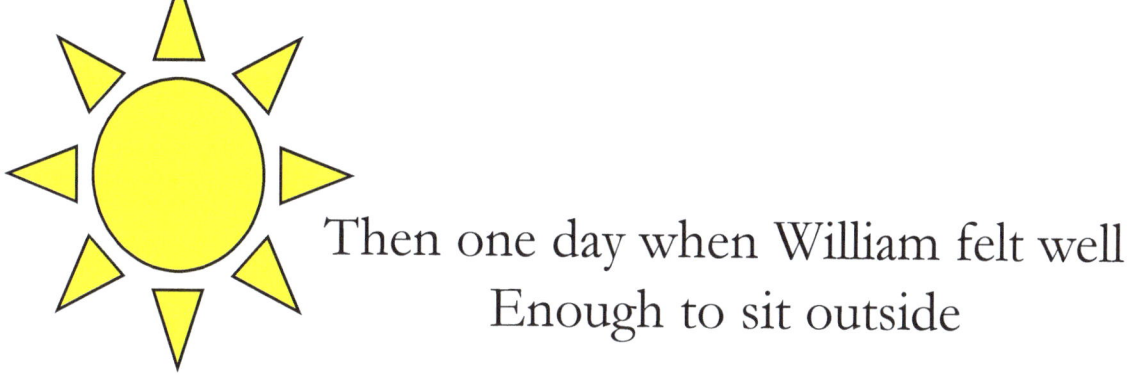

Then one day when William felt well
Enough to sit outside

He saw movement by the back gate.

It was a small gray tiger kitten.

Not sure if he wanted a kitten or not,

William did not invite the little kitten inside that night.

Nor the next.

And that was okay with the kitten

For he was not sure he wanted to live inside the tall white house.

He liked chasing birds and mice, being free, going where and when he pleased.

Every day the kitten came and visited William,

Sitting beside him as he read.

Or helping him till the dirt

And trim his bonsai trees.

On days when William was too sick to come outside,

The kitten watched him through the window

Making sure he was okay.

And their friendship

GREW.

William gave his friend a name.

PIPPIN

Soon

The cold winds of autumn started to blow.

And before long
The snows of winter fell.

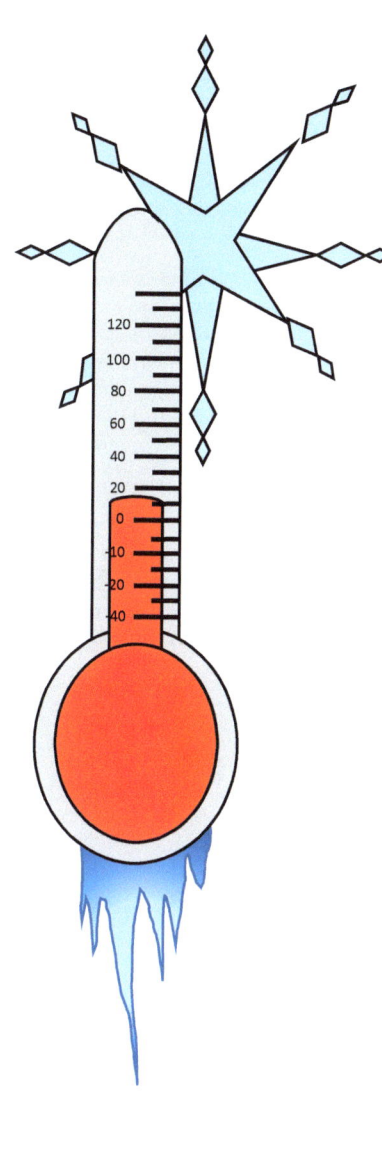

Pippin shivered and shook

In the cold.

Pippin had no home of his own.

He found an outside window well and curled up inside,
.
But it offered little comfort
And no warmth.

Pippin was cold.

Seeing how cold his friend was,
William invited him inside
To get warm.

Pippin ran right in.

Pippin stopped, staring ahead.

There stood the most beautiful thing
He had ever seen.

A Christmas tree.

Pippin knew William had made the tree
Just for him.

It was a "Welcome Home" Present.

Pippin ran over and pulled down a shiny red ball,

Chasing it around the room for hours.

William sat in his chair and watched his friend play.

He thought how nice it was to have someone inside.

Once more William was

HAPPY

Pippin was

HAPPY

That night, the two best friends shared William's bed,

Neither alone anymore,

Both happy and warm.

From that day on, the two have not been apart.

Each day they eat breakfast, lunch and dinner together.

On days when William feels well enough to go outside,

The two work in the yard

Or read a good book.

On special days when William is able to,
He plays jazz on his piano.

Pippin pretends to like the music.

He is always glad when William stops.

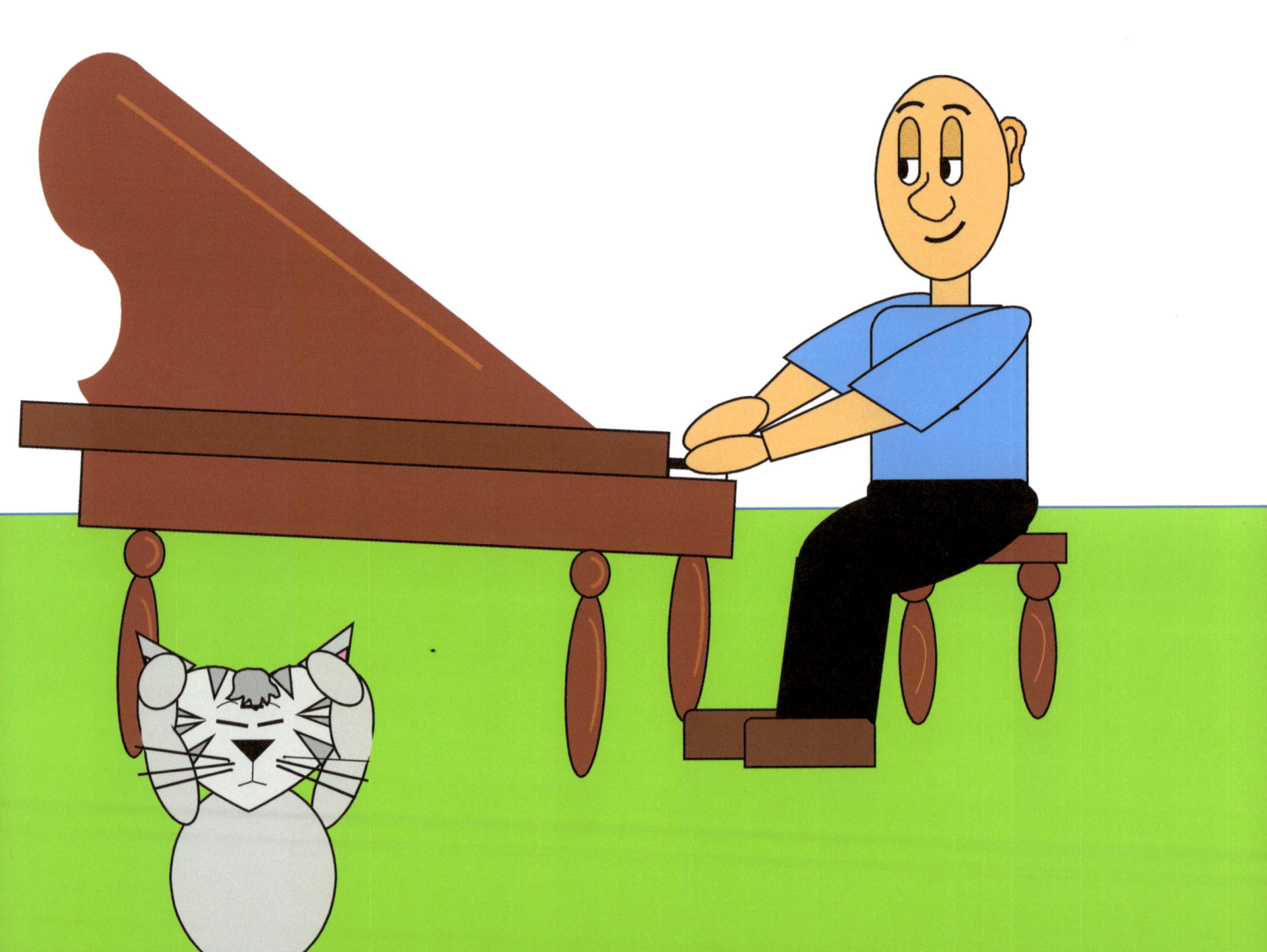